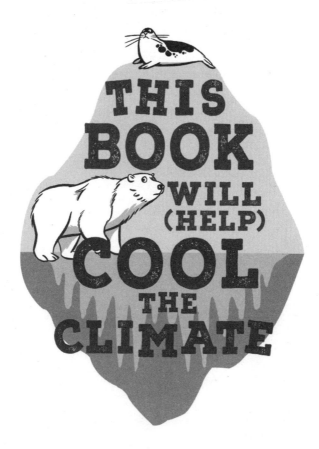

THIS BOOK WILL (HELP) COOL THE CLIMATE

First published in Great Britain in 2020 by Wren & Rook
Text © Isabel Thomas, 2020
Illustrations © Alex Paterson, 2018, 2020
Design copyright © Hodder & Stoughton Limited, 2020

ISBN: 978 1 5263 6241 4
E-book ISBN: 978 1 5263 6242 1
10 9 8 7 6 5 4 3 2 1

Wren & Rook
An imprint of Hachette Children's Group
Part of Hodder & Stoughton
Carmelite House
50 Victoria Embankment
London EC4Y 0DZ
An Hachette UK Company
www.hachette.co.uk
www.hachettechildrens.co.uk

Printed in England

MIX
Paper from
responsible sources
FSC® C104740

Publishing Director: Debbie Foy
Managing Editor: Liza Miller
Art Director: Laura Hambleton
Designed by Kat Slack

Additional images supplied by Shutterstock

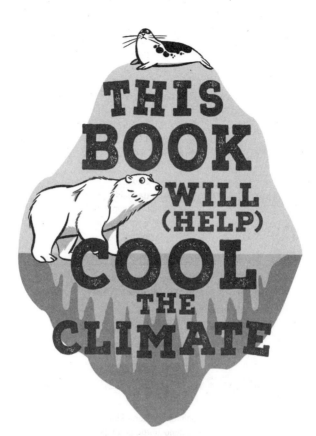

THIS BOOK WILL (HELP) COOL THE CLIMATE

ISABEL THOMAS
ILLUSTRATED BY ALEX PATERSON

wren
&rook

CONTENTS

QUICK GUIDE TO THE

PLANET-O-METER

SAVES:

WILDLIFE   PAPER/WOOD   ELECTRICITY   WASTE

RAINFOREST   POLLUTION   FOSSIL FUEL

WATER   FOOD

IMPACT: COST: DIFFICULTY:

KNOW YOUR PLANET

Knowledge is your number-one weapon in the fight against climate change. Let's start by finding out what's so special about Earth's climate.

PLANET-O-METER

If you could choose to live **ANYWHERE** in our solar system, you'd probably still pick Earth. While parts of our planet can get as toasty as 58°C or as ch-ch-chilly as -88°C, the average surface temperature is a comfortable 15°C. Compare this to Mars, with an average temperature of -63°C, and it's easy to see why we stay put!

Earth's temperature is 'just right' for living things, and not only because of our prime position in the solar system. After all, Earth and the Moon are roughly the same distance from the Sun, and yet from day to night the Moon's surface temperature swings between -173°C and 127°C. The secret to Earth's success is our atmosphere – the thin layer of air around the planet. This atmosphere is a mixture of different gases:

NITROGEN
OXYGEN
ARGON
WATER VAPOUR
CARBON DIOXIDE
NEON
HELIUM
METHANE
KRYPTON
HYDROGEN
NITROUS OXIDE
XENON
OZONE

Some of these gases – especially water vapour, carbon dioxide, methane and nitrous oxide – are known as 'greenhouse' gases, because they trap some of the Sun's energy as heat. Step inside a greenhouse and you'll notice a **BIG** temperature difference between the air inside and outside. The glass walls and roof of a greenhouse are good at letting sunlight in, which warms up everything inside. But the glass is bad at letting this heat out again. The air inside the greenhouse becomes so warm that it creates a different climate – one where all sorts of plants thrive. Greenhouse gases work in a similar way on a much bigger scale, keeping the whole planet warmer than it would otherwise be.

The natural greenhouse effect is a good thing. It stops the energy that reaches Earth from escaping back into space (like it does on the Moon), making life on Earth possible. Without the greenhouse gases in our atmosphere, the average temperature on Earth would be around -18 to -23°C!

But a few decades ago, scientists noticed something worrying. The greenhouse effect is increasing, trapping more of the Sun's energy than normal. Around the world, each of the last three decades has been warmer than **ANY** other decade in the last 170 years. In central England, for example, the average temperature from 2008 to 2017 was around 1°C warmer than the average temperature between 1850 and 1900. A similar 1°C average rise has been measured around the world. These aren't just the findings of one or two scientists, but **THOUSANDS** of studies.

Earth's average surface temperature rose by 0.85°C between 1880 and 2012.

A 1°C temperature rise doesn't **SOUND** too bad, but it's not just Earth's average temperature that's changing. Earth's water and weather cycles are driven by the Sun's energy. Global warming has already changed patterns of local weather conditions. Northern Europe and parts of Asia and North America have become wetter since 1900, with less snow and heavier rainstorms. At the same time, parts of Africa, the Mediterranean and Asia have become drier. In the Arctic (where temperatures are rising faster than everywhere else), less sea ice has formed every winter since 1979. Glaciers around the world are shrinking as their ice melts more quickly than normal. The same is happening to the huge ice sheets that cover Greenland and Antarctica. All this melted ice has to go somewhere, and between 1901 and 2010, the average global sea level rose by 19 centimetres.

Armed with these facts, you'll be able to explain to anyone that there's no doubt that global warming and climate change have already happened. But will the temperature and the sea level keep rising? To answer that, you need to know what turbo-charged the greenhouse effect in the first place.

KNOW YOUR ENEMY

When scientists notice something as weird and as worrying as global warming, they work as detectives to find out what's going on. If we think about global warming as a crime scene, they've found human fingerprints all over it.

PLANET-O-METER

Don't look now, but there are dozens of satellites zooming overhead, observing Earth from space. These Earth Observation Systems aren't watching humans (so you can carry on picking your nose); they're packed with tools to measure Earth's temperature among other things. Collecting data about what Earth was like in the past is harder, but it's still possible. The thick ice covering Antarctica and Greenland has formed over millions of years, and is filled with tiny trapped bubbles of ancient air. By drilling ice cores (long cylinders of ice) out of these ice sheets, scientists can test the trapped bubbles to work out what the atmosphere was like long before humans were around to moan about the weather.

The oldest Antarctic ice cores are around 3 kilometres deep, and date back 800,000 years. Comparing today's air with the ancient air found in ice cores proves that the mixture of gases in Earth's atmosphere has changed. There is more carbon dioxide, methane and nitrous oxide in the atmosphere than at any time since humans appeared on the planet.

Where did these extra greenhouse gases come from? Well, we know that carbon dioxide, methane and nitrous oxide are released by all the things humans have done to make themselves at home. Since the Industrial Revolution began around 200 years ago, humans have been burning vast amounts of fossil fuels (such as coal and oil) to power transport, industry, heating and electricity. When we burn these fuels, we release the carbon trapped inside them as carbon dioxide gas. We've also released greenhouse gases by burning forests and replacing them with gigantic farms.

Between 1750 and 2011, human activities released around 2040 billion tonnes of extra carbon dioxide into the atmosphere.

The evidence tells us that **HUMANS** are almost certainly the culprits in climate change. By releasing extra greenhouse gases into the atmosphere, we have increased the planet's natural greenhouse effect, warming Earth up. And greenhouse gas emissions continue to rise. A record 37.1 billion tonnes of carbon dioxide were released into the atmosphere in 2018. That's more than 18 times the mass of all the animals on the planet (including all the humans).

If we do nothing, global warming, climate change and its effects are almost certain to get worse. Use the facts to explain that we've all helped to cause the problem – so we all share responsibility for tackling it.

Time to
GET SERIOUS

DENY THE DENIERS

A surprising number of people deny that climate change is happening at all. You can help by answering silly statements with **SOLID SCIENCE**.

PLANET-0-METER

The evidence for global warming is overwhelming – it's hard to argue with a massive melting ice sheet. However, people disagree about **HOW MUCH** the climate will continue to change in the future, and the extent to which humans are to blame. A surprising number of people deny that climate change is happening at all, or that it's a problem. Part of the difficulty is that not everyone takes the time to learn about the causes and effects of climate change. Luckily, you can use these solid, science-based answers to set them straight!

'IT'S REALLY COLD TODAY, GLOBAL WARMING CAN'T BE TRUE!'

WEATHER and **CLIMATE** are different things. Weather is what you see when you look out of the window on a particular day. Climate is the pattern of weather over a **MUCH** longer time period. To help someone understand this, compare it to measuring other things, like how children travel to school. If you glanced out of the window only once, you might pick a rainy day and conclude that all children stomp grumpily to school under umbrellas. To find a proper answer, you would need to collect data from lots of children over a long time, and spot any patterns. Then you'd need to compare the patterns to data from previous years to find out if anything has really changed. It's the same with weather versus climate change.

'I LIKE WARM WEATHER — GLOBAL WARMING SOUNDS GREAT TO ME!'

Spending more time in shorts and less time in jumpers might sound ideal, but remember that the 1°C temperature increase is just a global average. In some places, temperatures have risen far more. And it's not just average temperatures that change. There may be a few places where climate change will bring benefits (such as being able to grow heat-loving crops in places that once were colder). But overall, the bad effects outweigh the good effects everywhere. Melting ice at the poles can lead to flooding thousands of kilometres away. Extreme weather events, such as droughts in the tropics, can cause food shortages around the world. It's not just humans either; the United Nations predicts that a million animals are already at risk because of climate change. We all live in the same greenhouse, and climate change is a problem for **EVERYONE**, whether you're an animal or a human, and no matter where you live.

EAT YOUR NEIGHBOURS

'Food miles' have been popping up in school textbooks for years. Should we ban bananas and other foods that are grown far away?

PLANET-O-METER

Food miles measure the distance food travels before it ends up on your fork. They were first used to highlight the idea that flying or shipping food from elsewhere in the world contributes to climate change, and that eating locally grown food is better. For example, chocolate has a huge carbon footprint – contributing 2.1 **MILLION** tonnes of greenhouse gases to the atmosphere every year – partly because cocoa from West Africa and the Americas has to be transported to chocolate-makers around the world.

> Eating a chocolate bar once a week emits
> 80 grams of carbon dioxide in a year – the same
> as driving 330 km in a petrol-powered car.

But food miles aren't as simple as they sound. For many foods – including lamb, beef, pork, cheese, canned tuna, eggs, tofu, rice and nuts – most greenhouse gas emissions happen **LONG** before the food leaves the farm. If local farms can only produce a certain food by using loads of chemicals (because the soil is not good enough), heated polytunnels (because the climate is not warm enough), gallons of water (because the climate is too dry) or lots of heavy machinery, buying that food locally may lead to **GREATER** greenhouse gas emissions than growing it somewhere else and transporting it.

At certain times of year, green beans grown in Kenya or lettuces grown in Spain are responsible for less carbon dioxide than the same foods grown in Britain in heated tunnels, harvested using diesel-powered machinery or frozen for a long time. Even chocolate turns out to be complicated – one study found that 60 per cent of the emissions for milk chocolate made in the UK is down to to the locally produced milk, not the cocoa.

So what can you do? Scientists at Harvard University, USA, recommend that we eat locally in **TIME** as well as space. Replacing food miles with food space-time?! It sounds like something we might need Einstein to explain, but it's actually pretty simple. It means eating local foods when they are 'in season' – at the time of year when they are ready to harvest in your area. This is when the farming methods and storage are more likely to be eco-friendly. What is seasonal when depends on where you live, so you could start with a bit of detective work by searching online. Collect pictures of foods and stick them on to a calendar in the kitchen to remind everyone which foods are in season that month. You'll also discover that some foods are **NEVER** in season in this country, so you could try to avoid those altogether.

TURN GARBAGE INTO GROCERIES

You can't get more local than food from your own garden, balcony or windowsill. Even better, you can grow it from things you'd normally throw away.

PLANET-O-METER

Learn to grow new plants from old scraps and enjoy free food that's good for the planet! Start each project on a sunny windowsill, reusing food packaging as pots (even old eggboxes will work). Potting soil is great for getting them started – you won't need much. Keep them well watered, but don't flood them. When the seedlings look sturdy, transfer them to the garden, or to bigger pots on the windowsill.

IMMORTAL CARROTS

* Line a saucer with wet cotton pads.
* Press a carrot (or turnip or parsnip) top into the cotton.
* Keep the cotton pads wet.
* Once the tops sprout, plant them in soil outdoors (or indoors in a tall container).

EVERLASTING GARLIC

* Pull off one clove from a garlic bulb.
* Plant it roots downwards.
* Put it on a sunny windowsill.
* When shoots appear, keep them trimmed.
* The clove will become a new bulb.

TIMELESS TOMATOES

* Wash and dry some seeds.
* Plant them in pots in spring.
* When the plants are a few centimetres high, move them outdoors (or move them into slightly bigger pots and keep them on the windowsill if the weather is chilly).

TINKER TRAINING

Buying less stuff is one of the best ways to cut your carbon emissions. But what if something breaks – surely you have to replace it?

PLANET-O-METER

If you picked up a gadget in a shop and the box said, **'THIS WILL BREAK DOWN NEXT YEAR'**, you'd probably put it back on the shelf, right? But incredibly, many of the things we buy really are designed to have a very short lifespan. This business model even has a name – 'planned obsolescence'. (Try saying that quickly like a tongue-twister and **YOU** might break down!) Some products, from lightbulbs and toothbrushes to washing machines, are designed to stop working after a certain time, forcing us to replace them. Other products, such as clothes, cars and mobile phones, are upgraded every few months or years. The aim is to make the old models seem clunky or unfashionable, so we want to buy a new version.

In 2018, the EU parliament voted to try and end the planned obsolescence of electronic gadgets. They want manufacturers to make products easier to repair, and to include information on the packaging about how long they will last.

Over time, if something breaks or looks a bit old, we've learned just to reach for a new one. It doesn't have to be like this. By trying our best to mend toys, gadgets and clothes, we can extend the lifespan of at least some of our stuff. It's great fun if you like to explore, tinker and create new things. And each thing you save from landfill also saves the greenhouse gases that would have been released by manufacturing a new one.

COUNTDOWN TO TINKERING SUPERSTARDOM

5. Before chucking something that is damaged – whether it's a remote-control toy or a pair of jeans – ask an adult to help you search online for a quick guide to repairing it. Try **fixperts.org** or **ifixit.com**.

4. Put your own tinker kit together at home. It could include a sewing kit and spare buttons (see page 76), a screwdriver and spare screws, a tape measure, pliers, tweezers, strong tape, non-toxic glue, safety pins, crayons, safety goggles, paper clips, elastic bands, scissors, string and a magic eraser sponge.

3. Get hold of some mouldable mending putty, like FORMcard or Sugru. You can use it to repair anything from broken shoes to a loose headphones lead.

2. If you're really stuck, look out for a repair café in your area (visit **repaircafe.org**). These often have tools and materials you can use to help you fix stuff, as well as volunteers to give you advice or even mend things for you.

1. If you get this far and something **STILL** seems beyond repair, why not 'hack' it to make something entirely new from the parts?

As well as shrinking your carbon footprint, tinkering gives you problem-solving skills that could get you an exciting job in the future. Just ask engineers like Danielle George, Jane ní Dhulchaointigh or Janese Swanson, who all loved fixing broken stuff as kids.

START AN ECO-LIBRARY

Libraries are awesome, and they aren't just for books! Imagine a library that loans out toys, fancy dress or party gear... then set it up!

PLANET-O-METER

Parties and dressing-up days are usually great fun, but our special occasions can put pressure on the planet. Costumes, decorations, cutlery, cups and plates are often used just **ONCE** and then thrown away or forgotten. To tackle this, communities around the world are setting up lending programmes that allow people to hire items for parties and celebrations. Your school is the perfect place to set up a scheme like this. Here's how.

1. Gather a small team to help you set up your eco-library, including at least one teacher or parent volunteer. Decide what you would like to loan out. Here are some ideas:

* Party decorations and reusable tableware
* Fancy dress costumes
* Toys and games
* Sports equipment

2. Get hold of your chosen items. The best way is to ask families to donate things they no longer use, or you could fundraise to buy things from charity shops.

3. Decide on the guidelines for rental. Where can families come to borrow items? How many can they check out at a time? How long can people borrow an item for? Will there be a small fee to join the library or borrow items (to fund new equipment)? What should families do if they accidentally lose or break something? Will they need to wash or clean the item before they return it? Include all this information when you tell parents about the scheme.

4. Plan where you will store items between rentals. You'll need strong boxes to keep them in. Make a list of what's included to stick inside the lid of each box. If you are lending toys or costumes, include information about which age group or size each item is for.

5. Set up a system to record what has been borrowed, when and by whom. This could be a simple printed spreadsheet kept in a folder. Even if you have only one thing to lend out (such as a box of party decorations), you will still need a calendar to record bookings.

6. As volunteers, your work is not done yet! Don't forget to check items between loans to make sure they are safe and clean to lend out again.

REWILD YOUR GARDEN

Good news – you can fight climate change by doing nothing!

IMPACT COST SAVES DIFFICULTY

PLANET-O-METER

From neatly mown gardens or fields full of just one crop to forests free from large animals, it can be hard to find an area of land that's truly wild. The rewilding movement aims to change that by leaving areas of land to return to a more natural state.

You can scale down the ideas for your own garden or a nearby patch of land. Focus on rewilding plants and the animals will follow. Just do as little as possible and let your garden get on with it! If you don't have your own space, persuade your school to let you rewild a patch of playground or playing field. You might not win any best-kept garden prizes, but you'll be helping to build a better-kept planet.

COUNTDOWN TO REWILDING YOUR GARDEN

5. **STOP** using chemicals. These are often used to control the plants and animals that would naturally live there. Persuade your family to avoid pesticides, weed-killers and artificial fertilisers.

4. **STOP** weeding. You don't need to buy wildflower seeds to get a beautiful wild garden. Just do nothing! So-called 'weeds' will soon find their way to your garden, dropped by animals and carried on the wind. If you let their seeds live long enough, they'll grow beautiful flowers – a great source of food for insects.

3. **STOP** tidying up. Let leaves, twigs and logs pile up too — they all provide hiding places for minibeasts and other wildlife. The more insects that live in your garden, the more likely it is that larger animals will visit.

2. **STOP** mowing the grass. Wildlife hates a neatly trimmed lawn – nowhere to hide, no flowers to feast on. Leave at least one patch of grass to grow long and wild, and only cut the rest on the highest setting.

1. **MAKE** a pond. Okay, this takes a few minutes of effort, but it's worth it to turn your garden into an exciting safari destination! Reuse an old plastic washing-up bowl as a pond lining by sinking it into the soil (choose a spot with some shade and some sun). Pop in a few simple pond plants to keep the water fresh and clean (leave them in the pots they come in). Then fill the bowl with collected rainwater and wait...it won't be long before wildlife starts moving in.

BE MORE GRETA

Teenage climate activist Greta Thunberg is single-handedly waking up the world to the climate emergency. Here are five simple things we can all do to be more Greta.

PLANET-O-METER

SAVES · IMPACT · COST · DIFFICULTY

GO GRETA

When Greta first sat outside the Swedish parliament carrying a sign saying 'school strike for climate', she wasn't a celebrity, a politician or a social media star. She was a shy teenager who says she often found it very difficult to speak. But by demanding that people in power listen to the findings of scientists and act for the climate, she started a movement that has inspired children around the world to act too. Greta was even nominated for a Nobel Peace Prize. More than a million people in 110 countries joined in with a recent school strike, but there are lots of other ways that we can follow in Greta's footsteps.

1. **Do something** – no matter how small. The scale of the climate emergency can seem overwhelming, but Greta's message is that, 'the one thing we need more than hope is action'. Taking positive action helped Greta to turn her feelings of sadness about the problems into a feeling that she could do something about it. The ideas in this book will get you started.

2. **Be inspired by others.** Greta's first school strike was inspired by students in Florida, USA, who left lessons to protest about the harm caused by US gun laws.

3. **Take the train.** No matter how important the event, or how long it takes to get there, Greta is determined to avoid fossil-fuel-guzzling flights. Instead of flying, she journeys around Europe by train or electric car. She even travelled by sailing boat across the Atlantic to attend a United Nations global warming summit in New York!

4. Spread the word. Greta believes that most people would happily help to tackle the climate emergency if they knew enough about it. Once Greta learned what the science said, she began spreading the word at home, persuading her father to become vegetarian and her mother to give up flying. Now she focuses on spreading the word to people in power.

5. Start now. You're never too young to take action of some kind. Greta was 9 when she began reading about the climate crisis, 11 when she decided to do something about it and 15 when she protested outside the Swedish parliament for the first time. There are thousands of ways to take action, and you don't have to do it alone – find out what's happening near you and how you can join in.

STAY OUT OF HOT WATER

To cut greenhouse gas emissions we need to burn fewer fossil fuels. Start at home by staying out of hot water.

PLANET-O-METER

Unless you happen to live near a hot spring, heating water is likely to be the biggest part of your carbon footprint at home. Some homes have boilers that burn natural gas or oil, roaring into life like boring rectangular dragons and belching out carbon dioxide, methane and nitrous oxide. Other homes use electricity to heat water. Electric heaters don't produce greenhouse gases directly, but most of the world's electricity is still produced by burning fossil fuels. In Australian households, electric water heaters produce up to **THREE TIMES** as much greenhouse gas as low-emission, fossil-fuel-burning heaters. Until more of our power is produced using renewable energy, using electricity to heat water is **BAD NEWS**.

Heating water counts for almost a quarter
of the carbon footprint of a typical UK
home, and contributes up to 5 per cent
of the UK's total carbon emissions.

5 TIPS FOR STAYING OUT OF HOT WATER AT HOME

1. Using a dishwasher can be more eco-friendly than washing up by hand, as long as you run the dishwasher only when full. If you have to wash up by hand, keep the water cool and never rinse under a running hot tap.

2. Swap baths for showers, but remember to keep them short. Spending more than four minutes in a fast-flowing shower can use up far more hot water than a bath.

3. Wear clothes for longer between washes. It will help them last longer too. Unless something is noticeably dirty or smelly, keep it out of the laundry bin.

4. Are you tech-savvy? Do people always call on you to get the computer working? Teach yourself how to programme the boiler too, so it heats water only when your family needs it.

5. If the water from your hot tap is always too hot to use, ask an adult to lower the water temperature on the boiler, water heater or storage tank. For most homes, 60°C is hot enough.

TURN THE TAP OFF!

If you're finding it hard to persuade your parent that you can save the planet by not washing your PE kit, remind them that all these tips will save your family money too. In the UK, around 20 per cent of the heating bill for a home with a gas-fired boiler is due to heating water for showers, baths and hot taps.

SAY NAY TO THE SPRAY

We often use aerosol sprays to make ourselves look and smell good, but for the planet, spraying stinks.

PLANET-O-METER

From hairspray and deodorants to spray paints, aerosol cans make it quick and easy to get liquids (and your hair!) in the right place. For a long time, gases called chlorofluorocarbons (CFCs) were used as the propellants – the gas that escapes when you press the button, forcing some of the liquid out with it. CFCs appeared to be perfect – they are non-toxic and non-flammable, so it seemed like a non-problem when they just drifted off into the air.

Then, around 50 years ago, scientists realised with **HORROR** that all the CFCs we were releasing into the air were drifting high into the stratosphere, where they messed with a gas called ozone. Ozone is a natural greenhouse gas, but it's also a vital sunscreen that blocks the worst of the Sun's radiation and makes life on our planet possible. The damage caused by CFCs had created a huge hole in the ozone layer over Antarctica. The problem was so bad that the world's countries quickly agreed to stop using CFCs and similar chemicals. The Montreal Protocol of 1987 became the most successful international agreement **EVER**, proving that countries can work together to stop environmental damage if they try. By the mid-1990s, the hole in the ozone layer had stopped getting bigger. We are hopeful that it will repair itself by around 2070.

The ban on CFCs was good news for the climate too, because CFCs are powerful greenhouse gases. However, spray cans are still on our shelves, and the hydrofluorocarbon (HFC) propellants used instead of CFCs are also greenhouse gases. One of them, with the deceptively boring name HFC-134a, is actually a supervillain 1,430 times better at trapping the Sun's heat than carbon dioxide! Each puff released from a spray can will hang around in the atmosphere for hundreds of years.

The countries that signed the Montreal Protocol have come up with a new agreement – the Kigali Amendment, which challenges countries to phase out HFCs. It would be a small change with a **BIG** impact, preventing up to 0.5°C of future warming. Some countries have risen to the challenge already. Others will follow from 2024.

However, not every country has signed up to the Kigali Amendment yet. You can help in two ways. Write to your local politicians asking them to take action to ratify the Kigali Amendment. Most importantly, avoid using aerosols yourself. Almost anything that comes in an aerosol **CAN** be delivered in other ways – sprays are only popular because they are easy to use.

TAKE A STAYCATION

Going on holiday can balloon the size of your carbon footprint. Give the planet a break by swapping your next family break for a staycation.

PLANET-O-METER

You've probably heard that air travel is bad for the planet, but did you know that a return flight from London to Rome has a larger carbon footprint than the average person in Madagascar or Ethiopia has over an entire **YEAR**?! Swapping a holiday abroad for a 'staycation' at home is a brilliant way to make a difference and can be super-fun too. Ban homework, cooking and cleaning and dip into this list of adventures.

10 TIPS FOR A
SUPER STAYCATION

1. See how far you can get by public transport (trains, buses, boats or trams) in just one day.

2. In your garden or at a local campsite, make a shelter you can sleep in, build a garden campfire and download a stargazing app for a night sleeping under the stars.

3. Plan a walk (or bike ride) using an online map and challenge your whole family to follow the route.

4. Do a tasting tour of your local town or city, visiting local foodmakers on foot and buying one thing at each to make the ultimate picnic. Then find a local park to eat your feast in.

5. Fill a jar with ideas about things to do (set a budget first) and pull them out one at a time during the staycation.

6. Try a new sport locally, whether paddle-boarding, paintballing or visiting a BMX track.

7. Plan a home-spa day dedicated to relaxation, reading and homemade beauty treatments. Try a sugar or salt body scrub, a cooling cucumber eye mask and a foot soak made with baking soda and peppermint tea!

8. Look for a local treasure trail or download the geocaching app and see how many treasures you can track down in a day.

9. Visit your nearest beach by public transport if you can.

10. Be a tourist in a town or city you know well. Start by visiting the tourist office to track down awesome viewpoints, hidden history and new activities. Remember to stop for snacks!

MEASURE YOUR FEET

When it comes to caring for our planet, we've seriously put our foot in it. Measuring your carbon footprint will help you figure out YOUR contribution to climate change – and what you can do about it.

PLANET-O-METER

Your carbon footprint tells you roughly how many tonnes of greenhouse gases are emitted every year as a result of the things you do. It includes greenhouse gases released by burning fossil fuel at home – for example, if your home has a boiler that burns natural gas or oil. It also includes emissions that happen far from your home, such as the greenhouse gases released by power stations that produce the electricity you use, by factories that make the stuff you buy and by farms that produce the food you eat. In fact, almost everything you use to do the things you do releases greenhouse gases at some point.

This doesn't mean you have to limit yourself to a life of long walks and sitting in the dark (though both are carbon neutral!). Some of our activities lead to far more greenhouse gas emissions than others. Calculating your carbon footprint is a great way to work out which changes you can make to have the most **IMPACT**.

Start with some detective work. Gather as much information as possible about the things you and your family do that use energy. If you find information for your whole household – such as the amount of electricity used each year – divide it by the number of people in your household to get a rough figure for just you.

THEN PLUG THE DATA INTO ONE OF THESE CARBON CALCULATORS, WHICH WILL DO THE SUMS FOR YOU!

CARBONFOOTPRINT.COM/CALCULATOR.ASPX

FOOTPRINT.WWF.ORG.UK

Once you've calculated your carbon footprint, compare it with the average for the country you live in and for other areas of the world (measured in tonnes).

QATAR 30.4
AUSTRALIA 15.6
CANADA 15
USA 14.6
SOUTH KOREA 11.7
RUSSIA 10.6
GERMANY 8.7
CHINA 6.7
NORWAY 6.6
UK 5.4
ITALY 5.3
PORTUGAL 4.9
SWEDEN 3.8   UKRAINE 3.8
INDIA 1.6
ETHIOPIA 0.1

DON'T FEED YOUR BIN

Food has an enormous (and very cheesy) carbon footprint. But you can start to shrink it without giving anything up.

PLANET-O-METER

It's not just burning fossil fuels that contributes to global warming – so do things like cutting down trees and raising cattle. Add up the greenhouse gas emissions from clearing and farming land, processing, packaging and storing food and transporting it to shops and homes, and you find that feeding the world's 7.7 billion people is responsible for a terrifying **QUARTER** of all greenhouse gas emissions. That doesn't even include the energy used to cook it.

But don't despair! It's possible to shrink your carbon 'foodprint' without giving up a thing. Instead of cutting down on what you eat, cut down on what you **WASTE**.

Food waste is a big problem. Around one-third of the food produced in the world each year never gets eaten. This means a third of the greenhouse gas emissions that stem from food production are contributing to global warming for **NO REASON AT ALL**.

The picture below shows how much of each food is wasted every year around the world.

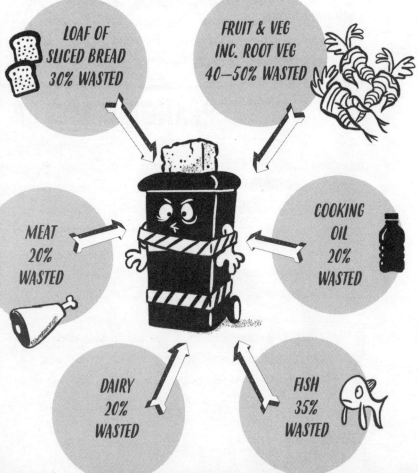

LOAF OF
SLICED BREAD
30% WASTED

FRUIT & VEG
INC. ROOT VEG
40–50% WASTED

COOKING
OIL
20%
WASTED

MEAT
20%
WASTED

DAIRY
20%
WASTED

FISH
35%
WASTED

COUNTDOWN TO TACKLING FOOD WASTE

3. HELP YOURSELF. Instead of being given full plates of food at mealtimes, ask your family if everyone could help themselves, taking only as much as they want to eat. This makes it easier to refrigerate or freeze leftovers for another meal.

2. GET CREATIVE. Once a week, challenge yourself to cook a meal or snack using only leftovers and store-cupboard supplies. Find some inspo online at: **bbcgoodfood.com/howto/guide/ love-your-leftovers-how-use-surplus- ingredients** and **lovefoodhatewaste .com/recipes.**

1. KEEP A DIARY. Whenever someone puts fresh food food in the fridge, make a note of the use-by date. If you haven't eaten it by then, freeze it! This even works with milk and cheese. (Cut it into cubes first.) (The cheese, not the milk.) (Cubing milk would be an udder failure.)

PROCRASTINATE FOR THE PLANET

As people earn more money, their carbon footprint increases too. Try this trick to stop your pocket money burning a hole in the planet.

PLANET-O-METER

Even within the same region or neighbourhood, individual carbon footprints vary hugely. In some parts of the European Union for example, individual carbon footprints vary from 0.6 tonnes right up to 6.5 tonnes. What are the reasons for this massive difference? Do people with a small carbon footprint live in special energy-efficient homes? Does their electricity come from solar power? No. Scientists discovered that the only important difference is in income.

The more money people earned, the bigger their carbon footprint grew.

For each extra €1,000 a person earned per year, their emissions increased by 265 kg.

It's easy to see how it happens. The more money people have, the more stuff they buy (particularly things like clothes and manufactured products) and the higher their emissions. So how can you stop your birthday money or pocket money burning a hole in your eco efforts? Try this simple trick.

Each time you want to buy something, from a new pair of trainers to a download, **WAIT A WEEK** before you make the final decision. A lot of the time, you'll find that the urge to buy fades and your procrastination will help the planet. (Plus, you'll have more savings for when you **REALLY** need something.)

GROW A FREE TREE!

Plant-saving, carbon-capturing solutions don't grow on trees ...or do they?

PLANET-O-METER

Although we need to cut greenhouse gas emissions, we don't have to reduce them to zero. Instead we need to aim for 'net zero'. This means that any carbon dioxide released **INTO** the atmosphere is cancelled out by taking the same amount of carbon dioxide **OUT** of the atmosphere. So how do we go about capturing something we can't see or touch? The 2015 Paris Climate Agreement talks about 'removal by sinks'. These aren't the kind of sinks you find in your kitchen. They include oceans, lakes and ponds, which naturally absorb carbon dioxide from the air. They also include the world's forests. Like all plants, trees capture carbon dioxide from the air and save it to make food for later, locking it away in their stems, roots and leaves – sometimes for thousands of years. So could we solve the world's climate emergency by planting more trees?

Scientists have done the sums and worked out that the planet could probably support almost one **BILLION** hectares of extra forest. These additional 500 billion trees would store more than 200 gigatonnes of extra carbon once fully grown, reducing carbon dioxide in the atmosphere by about 25 per cent.

Every tree helps – it doesn't matter if it's in the Amazon rainforest or in your school playground. By channelling our inner gardener and learning to take cuttings from trees that are already grown, we can all plant a tree for free and begin to balance our own carbon emissions.

Follow these steps to propagation power!

1. Find a native deciduous tree (or a climbing plant or shrub). Get permission from the owner to take a cutting.

2. Wait until the tree has just lost its leaves, or just before it grows new buds.

3. Find a bit of branch that has grown recently – it might be smoother than the rest of the branch or a different colour. Cut off the soft tip.

4. Cut a section of branch slightly shorter than a classroom ruler, cutting just above a bud.

5. Dip that end in a rooting powder – this contains nutrients that will make the cutting grow roots!

6. Choose a sheltered place (or a pot). Add some compost to the soil to give your cutting a good start.

7. Push the cutting into the ground or a pot, so that two-thirds is hidden below the surface.

8. Leave the cutting alone. Collect rainwater to keep it hydrated in summer. It may not do much for a year – all the action is happening underground.

STOP
RECYCLING...

...unless it's a last resort! Always focus on reducing and reusing first.

PLANET-O-METER

Many people have heard the mantra Reduce, Reuse, Recycle, but the last R always hogs the spotlight. It even has its own logo. Since the 1980s, recycling has been seen as a solution to all sorts of problems, from overcrowded landfill to plastic pollution. But the reality of recycling doesn't live up to its reputation. Each time we pop something in the recycling bin, we're not being as green as we think we are.

PLASTIC IS THE PERFECT EXAMPLE. It's not just a leading source of pollution. Plastic has a massive carbon footprint too. It requires energy to produce, form into products and transport to shops. At the moment, most of this energy comes from burning fossil fuels, releasing greenhouse gases into the atmosphere. Most plastic is also **MADE FROM** a fossil fuel (petroleum oil).

Yet plastic has never been more popular: 322 million tonnes were produced worldwide in 2015, and in the same year emissions from plastic were responsible for almost 1.8 billion tonnes of carbon dioxide – more than the entire country of Japan. Demand for plastic is growing so quickly that it will be responsible for 15 per cent of global carbon emissions by 2050 – that's more than air travel!

RECYCLING PLASTIC ONLY HELPS A LITTLE BIT. For starters, collecting, transporting, sorting and cleaning used plastic – and the recycling process itself – all gobble up energy and other resources. But most plastic doesn't even get this far. Only certain types of plastic can be recycled (or are profitable to recycle). It's usually cheaper and easier to make plastic from scratch, so over 90 per cent of plastic goes unrecycled, even if it's put in the recycling bin.

What actually happens to plastic waste in the EU?

39% incinerated

31% landfilled

30% recycled

At the moment, HALF of the plastic collected for recycling in the EU is shipped to countries outside the EU for processing. What's the point of cutting down on your own travel only to send your litter on a long-haul voyage?

If recycling can't get us out of this mess, what is the solution? We need to stop telling ourselves it's OK to grab a single-use plastic bottle, bag or straw because we'll recycle it. Instead, we need to focus on the other two Rs – Reduce and Reuse. Reduce comes first for a reason. Buying less stuff (see page 62) is the **BEST** way to tackle climate change **AND** plastic pollution in one go. If you **REALLY** need to buy something plastic, make sure it is reusable (or buy it second-hand, so **YOU** do the reusing).

BEAT THE JARGON

Understanding the science behind climate change is the key to finding solutions. Learn to unlock acronyms and decipher climate-change jargon so you'll always have the science on your side.

IMPACT COST DIFFICULTY SAVES 0

PLANET-O-METER

ACIDIFICATION

Oceans absorb carbon dioxide from the atmosphere. This can help to keep the atmosphere in balance, but it also makes the water more acid, which is bad for wildlife.

CARBON CAPTURE

Anything that takes carbon out of the atmosphere and stores it. Carbon sinks do this naturally (see page 65), but people are trying to invent ways to speed up the process. It's sometimes called carbon sequestration.

CARBON DIOXIDE (CO_2)

A gas in Earth's atmosphere which plants need to make food. It's also released when either plants or fossil fuels are burned. It's the main greenhouse gas that humans produce.

CARBON FOOTPRINT

A measure of the impact of something (or someone) on the environment, through the greenhouse gases they are responsible for.

CARBON NEUTRAL

When the greenhouse gases produced by certain activities are balanced out by activities that capture greenhouse gases.

CARBON OFFSETTING

Doing something to capture or reduce greenhouse gas emissions (like planting trees) in order to make up for something that releases greenhouse gases (like taking a flight).

CLIMATE

The pattern of weather conditions that is typical for an area over a long period of time – for example, the average temperature, or the average rainfall, or the average number of sunny days in a typical season or year.

CLIMATE CHANGE

A pattern of change in the climate of the world or a region of the world.

DEFORESTATION

When an area of forest is permanently cut down.

EMISSIONS

Greenhouse gases released into the atmosphere.

CO_2e

There are six main greenhouse gases, and our emissions are made up of different combinations of these. However, all emissions are usually measured in a unit called CO_2e, or 'carbon dioxide equivalent'. This unit describes how much carbon dioxide it would take to cause the same amount of environmental damage as a particular combination of these greenhouse gases.

FOSSIL FUELS

Coal, oil and natural gas, which formed from plants and animals over millions of years. They store lots of energy, which is released when they are burned, making them useful fuels. But burning them also produces carbon dioxide, a greenhouse gas.

GLOBAL AVERAGE TEMPERATURE

The average temperature of Earth's surface, measured by averaging thousands of different temperature readings from around the world, over long periods of time.

GLOBAL WARMING

A steady rise in global average temperature over a long period of time, which scientists are almost certain is caused by greenhouse gas emissions from human activities.

GREENHOUSE EFFECT

The way that greenhouse gases warm the atmosphere by letting sunlight through to warm Earth, then trapping some of this heat rather than letting it all escape into space.

GREENHOUSE GASES

Certain gases in Earth's atmosphere that trap heat and warm Earth's surface.

RENEWABLE ENERGY

Electricity or heat from sources that can be replaced quickly, or that never run out (such as wood and biogas, and tidal, geothermal, solar and wind power).

SEA LEVEL

The level of the world's oceans compared to the land.

WEATHER

The conditions of the atmosphere in a particular place at a particular time, including temperature, moisture in the air, cloud cover, rainfall and wind speed.

MAKE YOUR CLOTHES IMMORTAL

What do a T-shirt and a 123-km car journey have in common?

PLANET-O-METER

They are both responsible for 15 kg of carbon-dioxide emissions. For the T-shirt, just over half of this carbon footprint comes from the energy used for washing, drying and ironing, assuming it's worn 50 times. This means you could cut your carbon footprint by washing and ironing your clothes less often (result!). But you could cut it even further by buying fewer clothes – and making the ones you do have last as long as possible.

On average, we wear a piece of clothing for 2.2 years before getting rid of it. The most common reasons for throwing away clothes are because they don't fit or they are damaged and beyond repair (or we choose not to repair them). But it can be easy to make simple fixes.

Making each piece of clothing last just three months longer would cut carbon emissions from clothing by up to 10 per cent.

STAIN AWAY

If you have a pesky stain like tomato, mustard or grass, soak the stain in vinegar, then wash as usual. If the stain is really tough, make a paste by mixing vinegar and bicarbonate of soda and rub it into the stain with an old toothbrush before washing as usual. If the stain is really, really stubborn, sew or glue on a patch to customise it!

GET OUT OF A HOLE

If you have a tear or hole in the middle of your clothing, find a bit of scrap fabric to pin on the back, then sew back and forth over that at the front, to make the mend strong. No matching thread? No problem! You can treat each mend as an excuse to add a colourful new feature and customise your clothes.

COMING UNZIPPED

If a zip is stuck, rub a pencil along the teeth to loosen it. If that doesn't work, try doing the same with a bar of soap or even a stick of lip balm. If one of the teeth of the zip looks wonky, use pliers (see page 30) to bend it back into place. If the problem is a missing zip-pull, replace it with something else, from a paperclip to a fun keyring.

UPDATE YOUR PLATE

To prevent global warming, we must eat less meat. Happily, this is easy to do, and will make you richer and healthier too.

PLANET-O-METER

As well as gobbling up land, crops and water, livestock (animals farmed for food) have an enormous carbon footprint. Compare the greenhouse gas emissions released by getting 100 g of your favourite foods into your home:

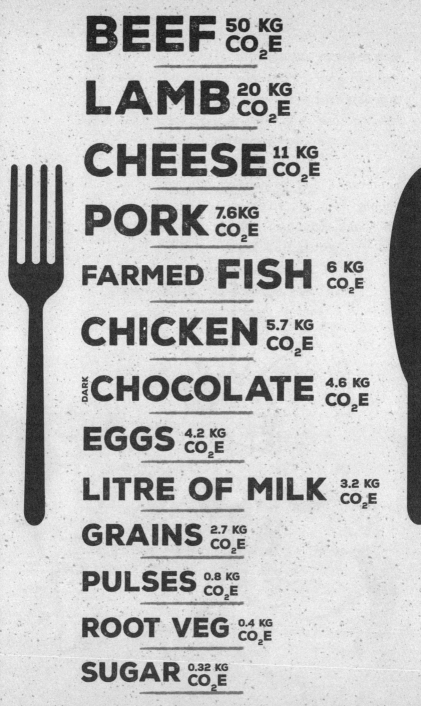

BEEF 50 KG CO_2E

LAMB 20 KG CO_2E

CHEESE 11 KG CO_2E

PORK 7.6 KG CO_2E

FARMED FISH 6 KG CO_2E

CHICKEN 5.7 KG CO_2E

DARK **CHOCOLATE** 4.6 KG CO_2E

EGGS 4.2 KG CO_2E

LITRE OF MILK 3.2 KG CO_2E

GRAINS 2.7 KG CO_2E

PULSES 0.8 KG CO_2E

ROOT VEG 0.4 KG CO_2E

SUGAR 0.32 KG CO_2E

Many people love eating meat, and all sorts of cuisines build dishes and meals around it. People also argue that we need the protein in meat. But we can get everything in meat from fish, eggs and plant-based ingredients (beans, lentils, peas, soya and nuts) too. After all, most of the animals we eat build **THEIR** bodies by eating plants.

Our bodies can't tell the different between protein from beans and protein from beef. But producing beef uses twenty times as much land and releases twenty times as many greenhouse gases.

Cattle are the real villains in this story. Nearly 60 per cent of all the world's farmland is used to raise and feed beef cattle, but this beef provides just 2 per cent of the energy in our food. As the world's population continues to grow, that land is desperately needed to grow crops for humans to eat.

A group of scientists has crunched the numbers and worked out that saving the planet means switching to a plant-based 'flexitarian' diet. This means eating vegetarian or vegan meals most of the time with only small amounts of meat, dairy and fish. It's a very different 'food plate' from the one we learn at school.

In some countries, eating flexitarian will mean introducing **MORE** meat at mealtimes, to ensure that everyone has fair access to a healthy diet. For people in countries like the USA, where people eat **THREE TIMES** as much meat as the global average, it will mean cutting back.

COUNTDOWN TO A FLEXITARIAN DIET

5. Begin by giving up meat for just one day a week.

4. On other days, try replacing some of the meat in each meal with beans, grains or vegetables – for example, by mixing lentils with meat to make burgers.

3. Consider giving up red meat altogether.

2. Learn how to cook vegetarian (meat-free) meals.

1. Going vegan (eating no animal products at all) can dramatically reduce your contribution to climate change but vegans need to plan their meals carefully to make sure they get all the protein they need.

TAKE IT FROM A T-REX

Digging up dinosaur bones isn't just for history buffs. The past has plenty to teach us about the present and future of life on Earth.

PLANET-O-METER

Prehistoric fossils aren't only good at attracting crowds to museums. They tell us all about past life on Earth – and not just who had the most teeth. We can use fossils to work out when different types of plants and animals lived and when they became extinct. This 'fossil record' tells us that there have been five huge extinction events in Earth's history – strange periods when most of Earth's plant and animal species... disappeared. All of these mass extinction events occurred at the same time as unusual changes in the environment, a big clue that we should take climate change seriously.

The most famous extinction event is the one that marked the end of the dinosaurs. It's thought to have been caused by a mountain-sized meteorite that slammed into Earth, filling the atmosphere with boiled rock and gases, or by giant volcanic eruptions that pumped carbon dioxide into the atmosphere, or both! This wasn't even the most dramatic extinction event. At the end of the Permian period, around 250 million years ago, more than 90 per cent of all plant and animal species on Earth at that time were lost forever.

Working out what caused this mass extinction is tricky (Permian archosauromorphs were really bad at keeping diaries). But all the signs point to a spike in greenhouses gases (caused by a giant volcano and methane-burping bacteria) which led to sudden global warming.

Scientists have found evidence that today's **HUMAN**-caused global warming may be contributing to a sixth mass extinction. Animal and plant species are disappearing 100 times faster than the normal rate, and a million species are thought to be at risk of extinction in the next few years. Life on Earth **HAS** recovered from previous extinction events, but this takes millions of years, and the world looks very different afterwards. It's something that all species would rather avoid – take it from a T-rex!

WEE ON THE COMPOST HEAP!

While you're rewilding the garden, you could try one of the world's oldest natural fertilisers!

PLANET-O-METER

IMPACT

COST

DIFFICULTY

SAVES

0

The fertilisers that many farmers and gardeners use are simply collections of nutrients needed by plants – such as nitrogen, phosphates and potassium. All these chemicals are also found dissolved in our wee! (When we eat food, our body takes only what it needs and wees or poos out the rest.) Scientists in Nepal did an experiment to find out if wee can help crops grow as well as shop-bought fertiliser, and the answer was a resounding **YES**.

A typical adult produces 0.8
to 1.5 litres of urine every day. Over
one year, this would be enough to fertilise
300 to 400 square metres of crops!

When fertilised with compost and human wee, sweet pepper plants grew taller and had more fruit compared with peppers grown using just fertiliser. Similar experiments with cabbage, tomato, cucumber and pumpkin plants have shown that veggies fertilised with wee are just as safe to eat. (The cabbage tasted normal too – phew!)

If you want to try it this trick in your own garden, follow these three simple rules:

1. Urine needs to be sanitised before you use it on food plants (usually by storing it in a sealed container for a month). If this is tricky to arrange, stick to sprinkling only on plants you won't be eating.

2. The scientists in Nepal found that wee works best when it's mixed with compost. This is exactly what one organisation, the National Trust, has been doing in the UK. So you could occasionally wee straight onto your compost heap!

3. If you are using wee on your flowerbeds, dilute it with water first. Very diluted wee can be used to water plants up to twice a week. Make sure you pour it on the soil and not on the plants themselves, as wee can be quite alkaline and salty, which can damage plants. Or mix undiluted wee into soil **BEFORE** you plant.

UNPLUG FOR THE PLANET

We're all drawn to the worlds seen in our screens, but spending our lives plugged in isn't great for the real world.

PLANET-O-METER

Science has shown that screen time ... isn't that bad for us. In fact, scientists based at the universities of Oxford and Cardiff have found that one to two hours on our computers, video games or smartphones each day may even be good for teenagers' mental wellbeing. It can help us feel in charge and that we're good at something. Lots of games involve creative problem-solving and connecting with other people. But the benefits of gaming come with downsides too. They encourage billions of us to spend far more than one or two hours a day plugged in.

A typical 8.8 GB game has a carbon footprint of 20.8 to 27.5 kg CO_2e, depending on whether it is downloaded or bought on disc. Most of these emissions (19.5 kg CO_2e) are due to the energy used while playing.

Swapping just an hour of screen time each day for an eco-friendly alternative can make a meaningful difference to your carbon footprint, so here are five things to do in a screen-free hour.

1. You don't need digital blocks to build a new world. Write or draw your way into your imagination.

2. Films and games absorb us because they make us care about characters. Start reading a new book series for the same feeling.

3. The feeling of perfecting a new skill is unbeatable. Teach yourself something that takes a while to master, like a sport, musical instrument or even how to do magic tricks. With an hour a day, you could be on top form within a year!

4. Do some real-world terraforming, by creating a small terrarium (indoor garden) or rewilding a bigger outdoor space (see page 36).

5. Round up friends and family and sample a different board game, card game or word game each week.

BREAK THE FASHION RULES

Strange as it sounds, fashion is all about making you feel LESS stylish. Break the fashion rules and save the planet at the same time.

PLANET-O-METER

Fashion gurus are masters at planned obsolescence (see page 27). By introducing new clothing designs every six months (or more often), the old ones quickly fall out of fashion, convincing us that we aren't stylish unless we buy something new. 'Fast fashion' is a genius way to get us to spend huge amounts of money on clothes, most of which we don't really need.

The world's
wardrobe is bigger
than ever – an
estimated twenty
new garments are
made each year
for every person
in the world.

Sadly, fast fashion has a shocking cost to the planet too. Textile production is one of the world's most polluting industries, with a carbon footprint of 1.2 billion tonnes every year. More than 60 per cent of these textiles become clothing. If you look at the labels of your clothes, you'll see that a large number are made in China and India, where much of the power still comes from power plants that burn coal. This boosts the emissions from clothing to 5 to 10 per cent of **ALL** global greenhouse gas emissions.

We can encourage our favourite brands to take action by making fast fashion unfashionable. You can start by never throwing old clothes away – sell them, pass them on to another family or donate them to a charity shop. And swap your own shopping trips for pre-loved style hunts.

THREE WAYS TO BUY PRE-LOVED CLOTHES

1. Ask an adult with a smartphone to help you sell and shop using online marketplaces, or apps such as Depop, Reshopper or Preloved. It's easy to search by brand, colour, size and style.

2. Hold a 'swishing' party or event at your school, where everyone exchanges clothes they don't like or fit any more for something 'new to you'.

3. Don't forget local charity shops. They get donations all the time, so drop in often for a quick browse. Don't be put off if an item needs a small repair – turn to page 78 to find out how.

SET YOUR SCHOOL SOME HOMEWORK

Schools are part of the problem and can be part of the solution.

PLANET-0-METER

The Australian Youth Climate Coalition is calling for schools to 'repower' with clean energy, by installing solar power systems on their roofs. This could reduce emissions by as much as taking 24,500 cars off the road! Not every school gets enough sun to use renewable energy directly, or can afford to invest in solar panels, but every school can do something to tackle global warming. Set up a green group at your school (this could involve staff and governors as well as pupils) and find out which of the following ideas might work for you.

Schools are responsible
for 2 per cent of all UK
GREENHOUSE
GAS EMISSIONS!

1. **Start a campaign.** Pick one or two ways in which pupils and staff could become more eco-friendly and start a campaign to get everyone acting this way. This could include things like switching off lights and computers, using less paper or choosing meat-free meals at lunchtime.

2. **Ask to learn about climate change.** Some schools are already building climate change into every lesson, and one area of northern England plans to train a climate-change teacher in every school. The more you ask, the more likely teachers and school leaders are to sign up for initiatives like this.

3. **Make school trips local.** Rather than taking a coach journey, visit somewhere on foot or by train. A day spent building dens in a local wood or a video conference with an astronaut might be more memorable than a trip to a distant museum. Or keep it ultra-local and invite speakers to visit you at school.

4. Take red meat off the menu.

You could start small with Meat-free Mondays or go the whole heifer and ask your school to ban beef. If you need inspiration, the catering department at the University of Cambridge has already stopped serving beef and lamb! See page 80 to find out why this is a good idea, and visit 0beef.com for a Change Pack to help convince your school.

5. Ban single-use plastics. Turn to page 68 to discover why recycling plastic is not enough. Instead, work out what your school really needs to reduce most. Ask each class to collect everything it throws away for a week. Focus on single-use plastics like glue sticks and drink cups.

DON X-RAY SPECS...

...to see through colourful labels and marketing jargon.

PLANET-O-METER

Believe it or not, food is responsible for almost **ONE-THIRD** of global greenhouse gas emissions, but not all foods have an equal share of the blame. Ultra-processed foods are some of the key culprits. These are foods that have been made using lots of different industrial processes, consuming energy at each stage. These processes change the foods to make them last longer or taste different – often by adding things like salt, oil and sugar.

It's difficult to visualise the carbon footprint of most processed foods – most of the emissions happen long before you take a bite. But there are clues on the labels that can help you work out if a food or drink is particularly bad for the planet. Once you know about them, it's like having **X-RAY SPECS** that can see through the colourful packaging.

5 CLUES THAT A FOOD MAY BE HEAVILY PROCESSED AND BAD FOR THE PLANET

2. IT CONTAINS PALM OIL.

Vast areas of rainforest have been cleared and burned to plant the palm trees that produce this vegetable oil. Deforestation is the biggest source of human-caused carbon-dioxide emissions after burning fossil fuels. It also means fewer trees are left to absorb carbon dioxide from the atmosphere. Palm oil is thought to be in around half of products on supermarket shelves and dozens of different names are used to describe it. Look out for these tell-tale ingredients: palmitate, glyceryl, palm kernel, palmate, palmitic acid, palmitoyl, sodium kernelate, sodium lauryl sulphate, stearate or stearic acid.

3. IT CONTAINS HIGH-FRUCTOSE CORN SYRUP.

This sugary syrup is made from maize, using lots of processes and lots of energy. It's often used as a cheap sweetener in fizzy drinks, and you might also spot it in breakfast cereals, salad dressings, yoghurts, peanut butter and jam. Using your X-ray specs, look out for the ingredients maize syrup, tapioca syrup, fructose, glucose-fructose syrup and isoglucose too – they're all the same thing.

4. IT CONTAINS SOYA.

Soya beans make their way into 60 per cent of processed food in all sorts of ways, including as flour and oil and as a preservative. Soya beans are also used to feed livestock, meaning that we eat soya indirectly through meat and dairy. Nearly half of the world's soya comes from Brazil and Argentina, where huge areas of forest and grassland have been cleared to grow the crop. This releases greenhouse gases into the atmosphere as well as destroying natural carbon sinks.

5. IT'S WHITE BUT IT COULD BE BROWN.

Bread, pasta, biscuits, cakes, noodles, crackers, tortillas and waffles are all made from grains such as wheat, corn and rice. They can be made from whole grains (using all parts of the seed) or from refined grains, which have been processed to remove part of the seed. Refined flours are often pale in colour, sometimes because they have been bleached. They require more energy and resources to make, so they have a bigger impact on the environment. Choose foods made with whole grains (e.g. brown bread, wholewheat pasta, brown rice) if possible – they are better for the planet AND for your body.

ASK AWKWARD QUESTIONS

When is buying stuff GOOD for the planet? When you harness your consumer power to demand change!

PLANET-O-METER

CLIMATE NEWS

Just 100 companies responsible for 71% of global emissions, scientific study says.

When you read headlines like this, it's easy to feel that you can't do much about the climate emergency unless you happen to be CEO of a major corporation. But remember, all of these companies are producing things for **US**. If we stop demanding these things, the companies will stop producing them. So, start demanding different.

One way to do this is to ask questions every time you buy something – and make choices based on the answers. This puts pressure on businesses to change, to provide what their customers want. For example, if everyone buying a digital device asked how much electricity it gobbles up while on standby, more companies would start to fit power-saving switches.

DON'T FORGET TO ASK YOURSELF SOME QUESTIONS TOO:

HOW OFTEN WILL I USE IT?

DO I REALLY NEED IT?

COULD I BORROW IT INSTEAD?

ACT LIKE IT'S AN EMERGENCY ...

... because it is! The time to take action is now, not in the future. Can you persuade others to think this way?

PLANET-O-METER

Emergency *(Emer-gen-cy)*

noun

a serious, unexpected, and often dangerous situation requiring immediate action.

Sounds like climate change, right? But at the moment, few people are acting like it's an emergency. We know what we **OUGHT** to be doing to tackle global warming, but it's easy to put it off until the future – perhaps because we look around and see other people doing nothing, or because **JUST ONE** car journey won't make a difference.

The problem is, 7.7 **BILLION** people are thinking the same thing.

In 2019, MPs in the UK parliament became the first in the world to declare a national climate emergency, inspired by young climate campaigners such as Greta Thunberg and the school strikers. They called on the government to take urgent and ambitious steps, just as they would for any other emergency. Other local, regional and national governments are following in their footsteps.

WHAT CAN YOU DO?

1. Find out if your local, regional or national government has officially declared a climate emergency. If not, contact your local representatives and ask them why not (see page 157).

2. Sign (or start) a petition calling on leaders to declare a climate emergency.

3. Set up a stall in the playground to share information about declaring a climate emergency with as many parents as possible.

Will it actually make a difference? After all, 'emergency' is just a word, and it doesn't come with a set of rules for dealing with climate change. Many people think it will. Declaring a climate emergency puts pressure on people in power to act quickly, and to put climate action at the top of every agenda. Language can be powerful – if people hear 'climate crisis' instead of 'climate change', 'dangerous' instead of 'polluting' and 'safe' instead of 'green', they might listen more closely, and be more likely to take positive action.

After all, it is an emergency. The United Nations has reported that one climate-change-related disaster happens every week, costing an estimated $520 billion of damage every year. In Greenland, melting sea ice as a result of global warming is changing people's way of life, affecting their mental health. In India, temperatures surging over 50°C have caused drought, leaving tens of thousands of villages without drinking water. It's not fair to wait until the climate crisis starts affecting you personally. Global warming is a global problem with global causes. Solving it needs to be at the top of **EVERYONE'S** to-do list.

TIME TO ACT

DON'T GET TOO DRAINED

What's the connection between a Mars rover, a remote-control helicopter and your Candy Crush score?

PLANET-O-METER

They're all powered by lithium-ion batteries! Better batteries might be a big part of a carbon-neutral future. These are already used in electric cars, but giant batteries may one day be used to store electricity generated from renewable sources, like wind and solar power.

However, producing, using and safely disposing of lithium-ion batteries gobbles up so much energy, water and other resources that some electric cars are currently responsible for more greenhouse gas emissions than petrol and diesel cars.

You probably don't have your own electric car yet, but taking care of the small lithium-ion batteries that power toys and digital devices can reduce waste and help to counter climate change too.

COUNTDOWN TO BEING A GOOD BATTERY OWNER

5. Keep them cool. Overheating damages lithium-ion batteries, causing them to stop working sooner. Try to keep devices below 30°C – avoid leaving them in hot places, like a sunny windowsill or a car on a sunny day. Take the cover off a device before charging it, and put it somewhere heat can escape easily (not shoved down the back of the sofa). And use fast chargers for only a few minutes at a time (they cause batteries to heat up more).

4. Avoid extremes. Charging lithium-ion batteries to 100 per cent then using them until they reach zero ages them much faster. This is because they have to work harder when the charge is low. Do small, regular top-ups that keep the battery between 30 per cent and 80 per cent charged all the time.

3. Be less demanding. Lithium-ion batteries in consumer products only last for 300 to 500 charge/discharge cycles until they die. Extend their life by closing all apps you're not using, so nothing is running in the background, and turning off Wi-Fi when you know you can't get a signal.

2. Take charge naps. Recharging batteries overnight can be a good way to use electricity when demand is lower, but keeping them plugged in once they're fully charged can damage them. If you have one, use a timer plug to stop charging after an hour or so.

1. Avoid parasites. Using your device as you charge the battery is known as 'parasitic load'. It's fine to check messages, but things like streaming a video or playing a game while charging is bad for your battery. Try to turn off your device while charging.

INVITE AN EXPERT

A visit from a local expert on climate change can help you understand the problems and inspire you to take action in new ways.

PLANET-O-METER

Ask someone to help you find out if there are any experts in your local area. Your teacher could also invite people to do a Skype visit. Here are some ideas for people you could try.

* SCIENTISTS BASED IN UNIVERSITIES, RESEARCHING CLIMATE, ENVIRONMENT OR GREEN POLICY

* CLIMATE CHANGE ORGANISATIONS OR BUSINESSES

* NATURE AND WILDLIFE GROUPS

* A LOCAL PARK RANGER

* THE HEAD OF A LOCAL GREEN GROUP OR REPAIR CAFÉ

* TEENAGERS INVOLVED IN CLIMATE ACTIVISM

* PEOPLE WHO WORK FOR ORGANISATIONS SUCH AS GREENPEACE

* ARTISTS OR MUSICIANS WHO ARE INSPIRED BY THE ENVIRONMENT

* JOURNALISTS OR AUTHORS WHO WRITE ABOUT CLIMATE CHANGE (HINT, HINT)

THEN PLAN WHAT TO DO DURING THE VISIT:

✳ INVITE THEM TO GIVE AN ASSEMBLY OR CLASS TALK

✳ GIVE THEM A TOUR OF YOUR SCHOOL, SHOW THEM WHAT YOU ARE ALREADY DOING AND ASK FOR THEIR IDEAS

✳ ENCOURAGE THEM TO HELP WITH OR LAUNCH A CAMPAIGN

✳ LET YOUR SCHOOL PAPER OR SCHOOL COUNCIL INTERVIEW THEM AND SHARE THEIR RECOMMENDATIONS

✳ RECORD A PODCAST TO SHARE ON THE SCHOOL WEBSITE

Once you've put their advice into action, remember to send regular updates, and inspire others to follow in their footsteps.

AVOID FOUR WHEELS

Cars are wheely bad news for the environment, but can you do anything about it if you can't even drive?

PLANET-O-METER

YES! Start by keeping a travel diary for about a month. Highlight every car journey where you were a passenger and the trip was (mainly) about getting you from place to place. For example, the school run, after-school activities and trips to see your friends or go to parties. Zoom to page 150 to read about alternatives to the school run, but skid to a stop on this page for ideas about reducing the carbon footprint of other journeys.

1. Start by highlighting short journeys where you could have walked, biked or scooted. Write down what stopped you, and some ideas for overcoming those obstacles.

2. You'll be more likely to use foot or pedal power if you feel comfortable and safe. Make sure your bike or scooter is in good condition – a bike shop or repair café may be able to check for you. Wear a helmet, and clothing layers that you can take on and off if the weather changes. There are plenty of apps and websites that will help you to plan a safe route, for example cyclinguk.org/journey-planner.

3. Walking, scooting and cycling can mean that you need to allow longer for a journey (though not always – the British Parking Association discovered that motorists in the UK each spend 91 hours a year looking for a parking space!).

If you're planning a longer journey on foot, use a map and see if you can explore a park, playground or new area on the way that you wouldn't see if you were stuck in a car.

4. For longer journeys, book in advance for cheaper bus and train fares. See if you can sign up for family or young person's railcards. They can save you **LOADS** of money. For example, if you go on holiday in Europe by rail, two children aged 4 to 11 can travel for **FREE** in 31 countries with an adult who has an Interrail pass!

5. For those journeys where you have to travel by car (such as a birthday party miles from a station or bus stop), try to share lifts whenever possible. It's better if one full car makes the journey than two half-empty cars. You can help to organise this by being the first to suggest it, and you'll end up with friends to travel with too.

CAST YOUR VOTE

A local or national election is a great time to tell the world what's important to YOU. Hold a mock election at school to bring climate issues into focus.

PLANET-O-METER

If there's an election on the horizon, your local candidates will be keen to speak to as many people as possible. Invite them into your school to talk about climate change. After everyone has visited, hold a mock vote. If it's not possible to invite candidates to visit, hold a shadow election with pupils representing each party and its policies.

1. **Send invitations**. The best way is to email the candidates or their offices (ask a teacher to help). Tell them your school is a part of their 'electorate' (the people who vote them into their jobs) and you would like to invite them to visit. Suggest a week that might work well. If you get no reply, follow up with a phone call.

2. **Plan carefully.** Work out how long each person will get to speak (make sure it is the same for everyone), and how long you will have for asking questions. Plan where the vote will take place, how everyone will cast their vote, and who will count the votes. How will you make sure the process is fair?

3. **Write questions.** Candidates will want to talk about lots of issues that aren't climate change, so it's a good idea to prepare some questions that you would definitely like answered. Do some research about each candidate first, and their party's policy on the climate emergency. You can ask them to send their campaign leaflets to make this easy – then ask questions that they didn't answer in the material. Here are some ideas below.

Are you doing everything in your power to fight the climate emergency?

What is your party's policy on energy and the environment?

What new policies would you put in place to act on climate change?

How will climate change affect our area?

What are you doing yourself to cut greenhouse gas emissions?

4. **Keep a record**. Task someone with keeping notes during the day, and someone else with taking photos. You could invite the local press along too and share the results of the mock vote.

5. **Stay in touch**. Write to thank everyone after the visit. You could ask them to support a particular campaign at your school. The support of people in power can be very important in getting things done. Follow up each time you have something new to report, or to ask about your visitor's progress in doing the things they talked about.

LIVE
S-L-O-W-L-Y

Too busy to read
this page? Then
you *have* to read
this page.

PLANET-O-METER

We use fossil-fuel-powered machines to speed up our lives: cars to
travel faster, gadgets to wash clothes more quickly, digital devices
to send information at two-thirds of the speed of light. In 1930,
a famous economist predicted that
machines would save us so much time
in the future, we'd need to work for
only three hours a day. But he was
wrong. Fast-forward 90 years, and we're
cramming more than ever into each day.

Work out how long you spend at school
each week, then add the time you spend
on homework, sports, music and other

organised activities. It's easy to see why sometimes you have to jump in the car or grab a bottle of water on the go, just to get everything done, right? The pressure we put on ourselves also puts pressure on the planet.

Now a whole movement is embracing the power of living slowly. Research suggests that not only are the following activities good for our mental wellbeing, they're also good for the environment. The less you try to pack into each day, the less you'll consume – and the more space you'll have to plan ahead and live in a sustainable way.

COUNTDOWN TO LIFE IN THE SLOW LANE

3. **Travel slow.** Try to travel by foot (or scooter or bike) whenever possible. For longer journeys, use public transport.

2. **Talk slow.** Try to only check emails and social media messages twice a day, and focus on face-to-face chats instead. A huge survey of 540,000 teenagers in 72 countries found that teenagers who spent some time eating or 'just talking' with their families every day were more satisfied with their lives.

1. **Think slow.** The internet gives us instant answers to our questions, but we could be at risk of information overload. Teenagers who spend more than six hours a day online say that they feel less satisfied with their lives. Swap some of your scrolling time for the slow pleasure of reading a good book.

SUSS OUT THE SCIENCE SUPERPOWERS

Keep studying science, technology or engineering and you could start suggesting new solutions.

PLANET-O-METER

Many scientists agree that we can minimise the effects of global warming if we can keep the concentration of carbon dioxide in the atmosphere at a safe level. But in 2019, the level started getting dangerously high and it's still rising. To bring it back down, we'll have to cut emissions **AND** try to recapture some of the extra greenhouse gases that have already been released.

How would you do it?

a) Line chimneys with glue that carbon dioxide sticks to

b) Use toothpaste as a sunscreen for the planet

c) Build a giant umbrella in space to shade us from the Sun

d) Snack on jellyfish crisps

Amazingly, these are all real solutions being considered by scientists and engineers! Chemists at the Energy Safety Research Institute (ESRI) at Swansea University, UK, have created a special carbon capture material using a type of glue found in most homes.

Scientists based at Harvard University, USA, are designing a sunscreen, using balloons to release tiny particles of calcium carbonate (one of the main ingredients in toothpaste) into the atmosphere, to dim the Sun's rays. Could it work? Well, we know that when a huge volcano erupted in 1991, the particles of sulphur dioxide it released made the planet 0.5°C cooler for about 18 months. Toothpaste is **WAY** less stinky.

There are worries that messing with the Earth's climate (even to try and do good) might have unexpected effects. So some scientists are looking further afield for solutions – such as building a giant sunshade in space. Other scientists are getting creative in the kitchen, exploring new sources of food such as jellyfish crisps (surprisingly nutritious), milk made from algae and flour made from crickets.

If this sounds exciting and fun, that's because it is. If you keep studying science, technology, engineering and maths, one day you could spend your time dreaming up and testing new solutions to save the planet. And you'll get first dibs on the jellyfish crisps.

GIVE SIGHTS, SOUNDS AND SENSATIONS... NOT STUFF!

Do you think you're good at choosing gifts? Think again. Science shows we're choosing all the wrong things!

PLANET-O-METER

More than three-quarters of us give objects that can be wrapped, but psychologists based in Canada have discovered that **EXPERIENCES** make far better gifts. People are more likely to react emotionally to experiences, from a 😲 sport, to an 😎 day trip to a 😟 film. This makes them feel closer to the person who gave the gift. Happily, these are the kinds of gift that make the planet smile too.

10 EXPERIENCES TO GIVE (OR ASK FOR)

1. TICKETS TO A FILM, SHOW OR EXHIBITION

2. A VISIT TO A PLACE LINKED TO A FAVOURITE HOBBY

3. A SPORTS TASTER SESSION

4. A TRAIN TICKET TO VISIT A NEW PLACE

5. AN APP THAT TEACHES A NEW SKILL, SUCH AS STARGAZING

6. A VOUCHER FOR A FUN ACTIVITY, SUCH AS INDOOR CLIMBING

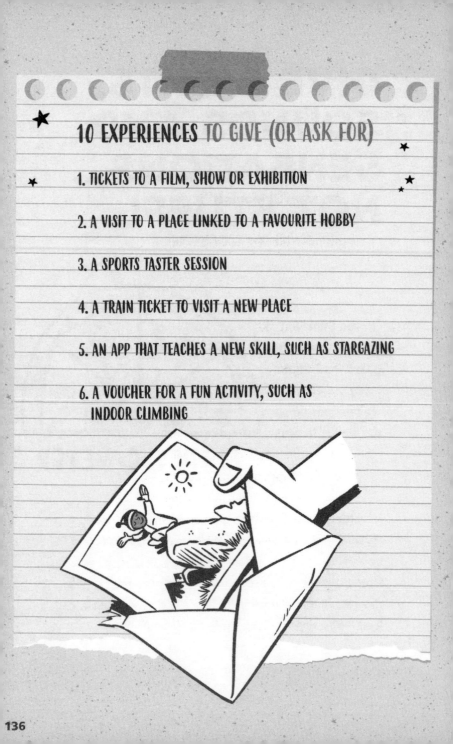

7. SOMETHING YOU OWN BUT DON'T USE AND STILL
   WORKS, SUCH AS A CAMERA

8. BICYCLE HIRE IN A COUNTRY PARK

9. A TICKET TO A SPORTING EVENT OR CONCERT

10. A CAMPING TRIP

Expensive surprises aren't any good either –
scientists in the USA have proven that people
prefer cheaper, more practical gifts. So next
time you're getting a gift for someone, tell
them you'd like to get them an experience and
ask what they'd like to do.

OPEN A MUSEUM

Entrance fee:
a pledge to help
save the planet!

PLANET-O-METER

Instead of visiting a museum, ask if your class
(or community group) can set up their own. Plan
a **MUSEUM OF CLIMATE CHANGE** event and invite
the whole school community. Appoint different
classmates to curate the exhibition, advertise
the event, issue tickets, act as gallery
attendants and even collect donations
to put towards a climate action project.

Several cities around the world have their own museums devoted to climate change, including Hong Kong, Rio de Janeiro, New York and Oslo.

Your exhibits could include:

- ✳ Info that explains the past, present and future of the climate emergency
- ✳ Everyday items that are climate change culprits
- ✳ Safer, greener alternatives
- ✳ Short films or animations you have made
- ✳ Art and craft projects to raise awareness
- ✳ Interactive exhibits, such as making draught excluders (see page 161)

Create a short information card about each exhibit and appoint different 'staff' to stand next to the exhibits to give visitors more information. Ask visitors to fill in a short survey on their way out to share what they learned about climate change.

Can you really make a museum out of recycling? YES! When Robert Opie was 16, he began collecting packaging that would normally be thrown away. He held his first exhibition in 1975. His collection grew and grew and became the Museum of Brands in London.

CLEAR OUT THE CLUTTER

We hate to say it but...it's time to tidy your bedroom.

PLANET-O-METER

Is your bedroom heaving with broken toys, games you've grown out of and gadgets you never use? Tidying up may seem like a one-way ticket to boredom, but the benefits may make you change your mind. Psychologists have found that people who think their homes are cluttered also feel more stressed. Clearing out chaos may make you calmer and happier. It may even make you more creative. Researchers in the USA discovered that children play **MORE** creatively when they have **FEWER** toys to choose from. Clutter seems to distract us from doing things we enjoy and care about.

So where does climate change come in? Clearing out clutter does two things. It redistributes what you don't need, so that others can reuse it. And it will show you that you can live with less, which will hopefully mean you buy less in the future. It can feel hard – we all get attached to our stuff. Break the process into steps to help.

Every year, more than £67 billion is spent on traditional toys and games around the world.

COUNTDOWN TO DECLUTTERING YOUR BEDROOM

5. Make space for two piles in your bedroom – one of things you absolutely have to keep and one of things that you feel happy to donate (including anything that doesn't fit, or that you've outgrown in other ways).

4. Turn decluttering into a game. On day one, choose one object to put in the donate pile. On day two, pick two objects, and so on. How far can you get?

3. Make a separate pile of things that are broken. Turn to page 27 to see if you can find a way to repair them.

2. Time for the feel-good part – choose where you will send the donate pile. You could try freecycling websites and groups (ask an adult to list them for you), local charity shops, collection banks, families with younger children, school libraries, playgroups or medical waiting rooms. There are also lots of apps for selling preloved clothes and toys – ask an adult if they can sell things for you.

1. Finally, sort your 'absolutely have to keep pile' into things you use often, and things you use more rarely. Hide the 'use rarely' pile away for a few weeks, then reassess. Is there anything you could now donate?

HACK YOUR HOME

Try these tricks to cut energy use and make your home more climate-friendly.

PLANET-O-METER

Time for some good news: in the UK, carbon dioxide emissions fell by around 38 per cent between 1990 and 2017. An amazing 18 per cent of the shift was thanks to businesses and households finding ways to use less electricity. This is something **YOU** can help with.

Just over a third of the reduction was thanks to a shift to 'cleaner' electricity, generated using natural gas and renewables instead of coal. (Natural gas is a fossil fuel too, but burning natural gas releases less than two-thirds of the carbon dioxide released by burning coal.)

1. **Vanquish vampires.** You won't need garlic. These vampires are devices that slowly suck electricity even when switched off. To stop them in their tracks, turn off computers, televisions, microwaves and other devices at the wall. Plugging everything in a room into one multiple adaptor makes it easy to turn electronic devices on and off with one flick.

2. Switch to the small screen. Most of us love to sit in front of the telly, and the bigger the TV, the more power it uses. Plasma TVs also use more energy than LCD screens. If you have a choice, watch on the smallest screen in the house. Turn the brightness and contrast down too. It's an easy way to use less power, could save your family up to £100 a year and may even make the picture look better.

3. Stop drying your sports kit on the radiator. It stops the radiator from playing its part in heating the house, forcing your boiler to work harder to make up for it. If it's a nice day, try hanging clothes near an open window instead (this saves on the need for ironing too!).

4. Adjust the thermostat by 1 degree. Heating and air conditioning is the biggest use of energy in most homes, and it's increasing in some parts of the world as extreme weather conditions make it harder to stay cool. Turning the thermostat up one degree (if you're cooling the house) or down one degree (if you're heating the house) is a tiny change that makes a massive difference.

5. Turn off the lights.

Okay, you can turn them on again.

PARK AND STRIDE

What would you do if you discovered the air in your school was anything but fresh?

PLANET-O-METER

You'd probably want to do something about it – especially as you're expected to breathe it all day, every day, while putting your brain through its paces. Shockingly, a recent report found that almost half of all pupils in the UK attend schools in areas where air pollution breaches guidelines set by the World Health Organisation. This means 3.7 million school children are breathing in tiny toxic particles that increase their risk of asthma and other health problems.

Traffic outside schools is one of the main causes of this air pollution. This includes exhaust fumes from the cars that collect around school on the school run. Twice a day, they make up an estimated quarter of all cars on the road! These cars don't just drop off pupils – they leave behind exhaust fumes that hang around playgrounds and paths.

RETHINK THE SCHOOL RUN

1. Take part in national or regional walk- or bike-to-school schemes, like Walktober in Australia. If that goes well, try a regular scheme to encourage more people to leave the car at home. This could include an informal walking crocodile (set up by parents) or a formal 'walking bus' (set up by your school), which follows a set route collecting new 'passengers' on the way. Or you could join in with a walk-once-a-week scheme such as WOW (Walk on Wednesdays) or Friday Footsteps in the UK. Some schools offer a reward to anyone who walks or cycles, like a free piece of fruit.

2. Help families that live further from school to take part. This might include lift-sharing or 'park and stride', where the school arranges for parents to use a local car park each morning and afternoon and walk the last ten minutes to school. You could even suggest that a walking bus or crocodile passes by the car park. The Living Streets website has everything your school needs to get started: livingstreets.org.uk/walktoschool

3. Persuade parents to change their behaviour. Lots of schools have found that pupil-led campaigns can really make a difference. This includes things like closing roads near the school for a day and even issuing parking tickets to parents. You'll need your teachers' help to do anything like this – never approach parents or cars on your own. Find out what other schools are doing and take some ideas in to show your teacher.

TACKLE CARBON PAWPRINTS

Pets may be cute, but they're leaving behind something gross.

PLANET-O-METER

And it's not what you think! Cats and dogs have a catastrophic carbon pawprint. The USA is the biggest pet-owning nation, and its 163 million dogs and cats are responsible for as many greenhouse gas emissions as 13.5 million cars. Just like the cars, it's not actually their fault. It's up to their owners to take steps to shrink them. (The emissions, not the pets.)

The biggest problem is their meaty (and fishy) diets. Producing cat and dog food is already thought to be responsible for at least a quarter of the environmental impact of animal farming in the USA. This is set to rise as more people around the world choose to own pets and to feed them better-quality meat.

COUNTDOWN TO CUTTING CARBON PAWPRINTS

5. If you haven't got a pet yet, **consider not getting one** (offer to take a friend's dog for walks or to care for it in the holidays instead).

4. **Always adopt a pet** instead of shopping for a new one. You could choose vegetarian pets, such as guinea pigs.

3. **Feed them green grub.** Ask a vet for advice on switching your pet to a less meaty diet. There are dog foods on the market made from insects, grains, root vegetables and even fungi.

2. **Reduce.** All the advice in this book works for your pet too. Buy things that last, avoid single-use plastic (hunt out biodegradable poo bags) and look for second-hand toys, scratching posts and beds.

1. **Reuse and recycle.** Make your own pet toys – there are lots of ideas online, and since they're free or cheap to create, you can change the toys more often to keep your pet entertained. You could even make your own cat litter using shredded newspaper or junk mail.

BE ANNOYING

Don't be afraid to pester people in power.

PLANET-O-METER

From world leaders to business leaders, Greta Thunberg has made headlines for speaking truth to power. At the United Nations Climate Action Summit in 2019 she told world leaders, 'How dare you continue to look away and come here saying that you're doing enough, when the politics and solutions needed are still nowhere in sight?'

You probably won't bump into world leaders very often, but you **CAN** tell your local politicians what you think. Start by finding out who your local Member of Parliament (MP) is. MPs are elected to represent the interests and concerns of people who live in a certain region (known as constituents). Even if you can't vote yet, you are still a constituent, so let your MP know about your concerns. The best way to do this is in writing. On page 159, you'll find a template letter to get you started.

MPs are responsible for debating and voting on new national laws. The questions they raise, the votes they take and the campaigns they support on your behalf can make a big difference. Once a new law has been passed, the responsibility for putting it into action may lie with regional or local governments, so getting in touch with local politicians can make a difference too. Ask your teacher to help find out who your local politicians are and use the tips on page 126 to invite them to talk to your class and answer your questions. Remember to ask how **YOU** can get involved in local politics yourself one day!

LETTERS FOR CHANGE

Use the template letter overleaf to begin writing your own letter to a politician.

PLANET-O-METER

You can adapt this to write to anyone in power at the local, regional or national level. To help your letter stand out, keep it short (one side of A4), be polite and include your name and school address so they can see that you are their constituent. As with any piece of writing, start with **RESEARCH**. Find out as much as you can about the issue you are concerned about, the science behind it and whether the politician has already done any work linked to it.

Remember to end your letter by asking them to take **ACTION** – the more specific the better! For example, would you like them to bring something up in parliament or raise it with the government department responsible for climate change, to vote in a particular way on a proposed new law, to help you campaign on a local issue, or to do something else?

The larger the area a politician represents, the more constituents they will have. For an MP, this can be in the tens of thousands. They may get hundreds of letters every day. But they say that personal letters (or emails) really do make a difference. The more letters and emails they receive, the better they will understand what matters to their constituents.

[Your address]

[Their address]

[Date]

Dear [Name and title]

I am writing to you about the climate emergency. We urgently need to reduce greenhouse gas emissions in our country and around the world.

[Add a few sentences about your personal story (see page 180) and what you are especially worried about. How does climate change affect you and your local area now, or how will it affect you in the future? Let them know any actions you are taking yourself.

You could also mention any scientific findings or headlines that have worried you.

Ask them to take action on this issue (be specific!).]

I look forward to hearing back from you.

Yours sincerely,

[Your name]

HOW TO GET IN TOUCH

Ask an adult to help you find the right postal or email address. Most countries have special websites with listings, for example:

AUSTRALIA:
APH.GOV.AU/SENATORS_AND_MEMBERS/GUIDELINES_
FOR_CONTACTING_SENATORS_AND_MEMBERS

INDIA:
LOKSABHAPH.NIC.IN/MEMBERS/ALPHABETICALLIST.ASPX

UK:
PARLIAMENT.UK/MPS-LORDS-AND-OFFICES/MPS/

FILL YOUR HOME WITH SNAKES

Not real ones!
These rag reptiles
only prey on
draughts.

PLANET-O-METER

Picture this. You're snuggled up on the sofa, remote control in one hand, popcorn in the other, ready to hit play. Suddenly something **COLD** and **UNWELCOME** sends a shiver down your spine. Draughts are those annoying currents of cold air that waft through rooms, making it feel colder than it really is. They mean warm air is escaping from our homes and they get us reaching for the thermostat, nudging up our energy use even further.

Draught-proofing is your secret weapon in saving energy, and the easiest way to do it is to fill the house with snakes. These serpent-shaped draught excluders are easy to make using things that you might otherwise throw away, and perfect for blocking small gaps under windows and doors. For stuffing you can use anything you have around the house. Use a mixture of **HEAVY** things (such as gravel, rice, dried beans, peas or corn) and **SOFT, FLUFFY** things (such as scrap packaging from deliveries, the insides of a really old pillow or cushion, old tights and socks, used plastic bags or a rolled-up blanket).

The Energy Saving Trust worked out that
UK households could save at least £20
a year by ~~making novelty snakes~~ blocking
draughts at doors and windows.

SEW A SNAKE

☆ Cut one leg off a worn pair of trousers or tights. (Ask a parent first.) (Especially if they're wearing the trousers or tights.)

☆ Tie one end with a strip of fabric or a scrap of string or ribbon.

☆ Fill the leg with stuffing, packing it really tightly.

☆ Tie the end.

☆ Glue or sew on button eyes and a red ribbon or fabric tongue.

SUPER-QUICK SOFTY SNAKE

Do you have loads of soft toys you can't bear to part with? Give them a job saving the planet! Simply line them up with their backs against a door or wall. Then safety-pin them together to make soft toy 'snake'.

Don't block holes that are supposed to be there, such as air bricks, window vents and extractor fans. They keep the air in our homes fresh and healthy.

MARCH FOR THE CLIMATE

Would you like to protest in person? Don't leave home without reading these tips!

PLANET-O-METER

Since Greta Thunberg's first protest outside the Swedish parliament (see page 41), thousands of young people in more than 1,500 cities around the world have joined in with climate marches, protests and strikes. If you are planning to join in, read this first so you go prepared.

COUNTDOWN TO A MEANINGFUL MARCH

5. Know what you're marching for. People have responded very differently to the news that thousands of children are taking action for the climate. In one English school, the headteacher asked pupils questions to prove they knew what they were marching for. Read up on the event and the issues it is drawing attention to before you sign up.

4. **Plan carefully.** Many climate change protests are planned as peaceful and quiet protests, and some (such as many #FridaysforFuture events) seek police approval in advance. The organisers should help by providing details on a website or flyer. Research where they plan to meet, what people will do once they are there (for example, walking along a planned route, taking part in activities, or listening to speeches and music), and how they plan to keep protestors safe (for example, by organising for roads to be closed).

3. **Invite your friends and family.** Never go to a protest alone. Taking an adult along with you will help keep you safe – and anyway, the more people who show up, the louder the message. So invite friends and family to go along.

2. **Make a placard.** A protest sign helps you share your message with the world. Make yours from recycled materials and try to make it rain-proof. See if there are any rules for the event you are attending – some don't allow signs on sticks. Keep your message short and snappy so you can write it big – that way it will be seen from a distance.

1. **Stay safe.** Plan how you will travel to and from the protest, and what you will do if you get separated from your friends and family. If the crowd is very large, mobile phones may not work as well as usual. You might be standing for a long time, so wear comfortable shoes and dress for the weather. Remember water, snacks and any medicines you need. When any large group of people gathers, unexpected things can sometimes happen. Stick closely together and be prepared to leave if some people aren't behaving peacefully.

SWAP YOUR STUFF

**Free stuff?
Yes please!**

PLANET-O-METER

It feels good to get something new, but the feeling doesn't last for long. Psychologists have found that the joy fades away over as little as **FIVE** days. Soon a new toy or game catches our eye and the cycle repeats itself. The cost to the planet is huge.

To get that 'new-to-you' feeling without hurting your purse or your planet, try organising a swap party or event. It could reduce waste that might otherwise end up in landfill, help you to declutter your bedroom (see page 141) **AND** cut the amount of new stuff being bought.

1. **Pick a location** with a large captive audience, such as school, or a group that you belong to. You'll need a room large enough to lay things out with space for people to walk around and 'shop'. You'll need to recruit several adult helpers too.

2. **Set the ground rules.** For example, you could ask that all donated toys, books and games are clean and unbroken, with no missing pieces. You could also ask people to avoid donating electrical or battery-powered toys (or at least remove the batteries first).

3. **Decide on a system.** Reuse scrap materials to make tokens, which will work like money at the event. You could issue one 'token' per toy, so each person can choose the same number of toys as they donated. But it's not fair to swap a scooter for a soft toy! Why not ask someone like a teacher or parent to decide on the 'value' of each item, and issue tokens accordingly?

4. **Spread the word.** Make posters and ask if your event can be featured in school or local newsletters. Include information about when and where to bring toys along for tagging, and when to turn up for the swap itself. Remember to ask people to bring their own bags to carry their swaps away in.

5. **Ready, steady, swap!** On the day, leave plenty of time for checking donations, making sure they are clean and safe, and tagging them with a 'price'. You could designate a certain table for each 'price' – for example, 2 tokens, 5 tokens, 10 tokens. This is quicker than tagging each toy, but you'll need someone on each table to collect the tokens. If there are items left at the end, you could donate them or save them for a future swap event.

READY, STEADY, SWAP!

LEAD BY EXAMPLE...

FOLLOW ME!

Are leaders born or made?

PLANET-O-METER

SAVES · IMPACT · COST · DIFFICULTY

Research shows that everyone has the potential to develop leadership skills. Taking action against something you care about – like climate change – can be a great way to get started.

Start by brainstorming all the things that make you, **YOU**! If you're not sure what to write down, try snipping pictures and words from old magazines and newspapers to make a collage that represents you. Now scribble down all the qualities from your collage that could make a difference in your work for climate change. Are you excellent at research, talented at telling stories or keen on arts and crafts? Brainstorm ways that you could put your special skills and qualities to work to raise awareness about environmental issues. This exercise might help you pick which things in this book you'd like to try.

Next, write down the names of some people that you could tell about each idea, or even ask to help or support you. Now you have a plan. Finally, take a deep breath, get out there and start sharing your ideas. Lead by example, and you'll inspire other people to follow in your footsteps without having to boss them around. This is leadership – you are doing it!

HUNT FOR YOUR HERO

With so many ways to help the planet, where should you start? Take a tip from other young climate activists and be guided by your interests and skills.

PLANET-O-METER

Young climate activists are making headlines around the world with their action against climate change. Complete the quiz on the next page to find out which eco-hero you have most in common with, then find out how they got started.

1. What is one aspect of climate change you feel very concerned about?

a) Climate injustice – when the effects of climate change (and the responsibility for tackling it) are not fairly shared

b) The increased risk of devastating famines

c) Extreme weather events

d) The impact on the world's oceans and their wildlife

2. What special talents or skills do you have?

a) Theatre skills and singing

b) Giving speeches in front of lots of people

c) Being strong, through things like sports and circus skills

d) Technical skills like making films

3. What gives you hope?

a) When children realise how powerful they can be

b) When people put the climate above their own desires

c) Being part of positive action like a rally

d) Discovering simple things I can do that really make a difference

4. What is one change you would really to see?

a) 100 per cent renewable energy by 2030

b) News sites reporting on the climate crisis more than celebrity news

c) An end to new coal, oil or gas projects

d) People leading sustainable lives and creating less waste

Mostly As
Your climate hero might be ...
Noga Levy-Rapoport
Noga lives in the UK, where she juggles her schoolwork with helping to lead the UK Student Climate Network. As a young climate activist, she campaigns for politicians to take climate change more seriously. As well as writing articles and speaking at rallies and on the radio, Noga helps to organise the school strike for climate marches in the United Kingdom and has led a protest march in London.

Mostly Bs
Your climate hero might be ... Leah Namugerwa
Leah lives in Uganda, a country where the higher average temperatures caused by global warming are leading to more severe droughts and the desertification of farming land. Leah was inspired to take action when she was 12 and saw news reports about a famine affecting millions of people in the north of her country. Leah takes part in school strikes through Fridays for Future Uganda and organised a petition to ban plastic bags in Uganda. She also leads by example, planting 200 trees for her fifteenth birthday instead of having a party.

Mostly Cs
Your climate hero might be ...
Harriet O'Shea Carre

Together with her friends Milou Albrecht and Callum Bridgefoot, Harriet started the Australian School Strike for Climate (SS4C) movement in 2018. They led the first strike outside their local MP's office, demanding an end to new fossil fuel projects and a commitment to 100 per cent renewable energy by 2030. Harriet says that talking to politicians is out of her comfort zone, but that it's worth it to try and get people to take action for a safe planet. She was invited to share her vision at the United Nations Youth Climate Summit.

Mostly Ds
Your climate hero might be ...
Dylan D'Haeze

Dylan was 13 when he first became aware of the huge problems caused by plastic waste in the world's oceans. At first, he felt worried, but he decided to tackle his worries by asking questions and learning how to make films to share the answers he discovered. Since then, Dylan has made a whole series of documentaries to share the problems of climate change with other children around the world. You can watch them at kidscansavetheplanet.com.

These stories show there is more than **ONE** way to fight for the climate. Start with the issues that concern you most and think about how you can use your unique talents and skills to share the message – and inspire people to find solutions.

DON'T TRY TO BE PERFECT

It's better to take small steps than to do nothing at all.

PLANET-O-METER

The best leaders don't expect to get their own way all the time, and they don't want to. Instead, they share their vision and ideas, then listen carefully to other people. They hope to inspire other people to have their own ideas and take action too.

What should you do if someone criticises your ideas? Climate activists find this can happen, partly because taking action means making changes to the way we live. Some of these changes will be inconvenient – for individuals, for businesses and for people in power. But climate scientists want us to start thinking differently. They argue that short-term inconveniences are nothing compared to the risks of overheating our planet.

By researching the science behind climate change and potential solutions, you can listen to other points of view, but be confident in your own understanding and ideas. Most importantly, don't feel that you have to live a 'perfect', zero-carbon life before you can start encouraging other people to take action. Sometimes famous climate-change campaigners are criticised for doing things that use fossil fuels, such as taking flights. There is no such thing as a truly zero-carbon life at the moment, but that doesn't mean we should stop working towards it. It's far better to have millions of people doing climate action imperfectly than to have just a handful trying to live a zero-carbon life while everyone else does nothing at all.

SHARE A STORY

Once upon a time there was a planet that was not too hot, not too cold but just right...

PLANET-O-METER

The science of climate change is really important. Gathering huge amounts of data over a vast area and thousands of years is the only way to fully understand what is happening. But stories can tell us why climate change **MATTERS**.

Many people respond more emotionally to stories than statistics, so storytelling can be a powerful way to connect with people about climate change.

If you're excellent at entertaining people with anecdotes or brilliant at building suspense, consider using your storytelling skills to tackle the climate emergency.

Stories get people talking. Two not-for-profit organisations – the Environmental Defense Fund and The Hunger Project – made a Bollywood-style film called *Aarohan* about the challenges of climate change for rural communities in India, such as access to food and water. It's being used to get communities talking about different ideas for fighting climate change.

GET TALKING

5 IDEAS FOR FIGHTING CLIMATE CHANGE WITH STORYTELLING

1. **What's your story?** When did you first learn about climate change, and how did it make you feel? What are you doing to make a difference? How has it made you feel? Practise telling it, in words, in writing or in another creative way – for example, as a cartoon or comic strip.

2. **Tell the story of climate change in your own words.** It's epic. Who and what are the villains? Who will be the heroes?

3. **Dig out local stories.** Climate change is a global problem, which can often mean numbers so big they're hard to understand or care about. Telling someone about the impact of climate change on a nearby person, animal or plant can make them sit up and listen.

4. **Share happy stories too.** The stories of climate change that make headlines often leave us feeling scared, frustrated or powerless. But people are more likely to take action if they feel hopeful. When you read a story about positive action by a person, organisation or government, share it with others.

5. Start a new chapter. Remember that the story of climate change is still being written, and you get to help decide how it ends.

GREEN, SLEEP, REPEAT

Climate action isn't just about breaking bad habits...

PLANET-O-METER

...it's about forming new ones that last for life. Some of the changes in this book (like rewilding a garden) are one-off projects. But most are small changes to the way you live that will help you help the planet forever. Luckily, science tells us how to form a habit that lasts.

1. **Give yourself a cue.** Tack a new task on to something you **ALREADY** do every day and it will soon become automatic too. For example, you could decide that 'each time I head to the bathroom to brush my teeth, I'll turn off every socket and device I pass on my way'.

2. **Take two months.** Scientists at University College London studied 96 different people and found they took an average of 66 days to form a new habit. Expect it to take this long to make a new habit part of your life, and don't try to make 50 changes at once, or it might be your brain that overheats!

3. **Don't worry if you miss a day.** The University College London study also found that slipping up didn't stop people forming a habit if they just kept going as normal afterwards. Having a barbecued burger or doing the school run by car because it's pouring with rain doesn't mean you've failed. It means you're on the right path, because you've started to notice what you do and the impact it has on the environment.

IF THE PLANET HAD ANOTHER 7.7 BILLION PEOPLE **LIKE YOU,** ITS PROBLEMS WOULD BE **SOLVED.**

INDEX

ALSO AVAILABLE FROM WREN & ROOK

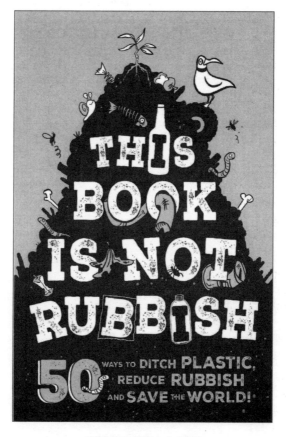

978 1 5263 6153 0 | £6.99

ALSO AVAILABLE FROM WREN & ROOK

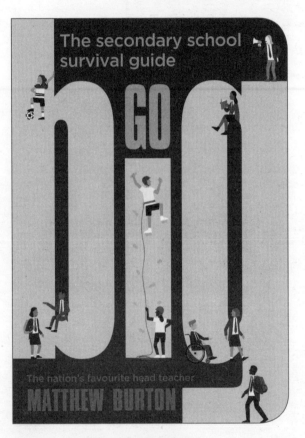

The secondary school survival guide

GO BIG

The nation's favourite head teacher

MATTHEW BURTON

978 1 5263 6235 3 | £7.99